A SECOND
GOLDEN
TREASURY
OF
CHILDREN'S
VERSE

A SECOND
GOLDEN
TREASURY
—— OF ——
CHILDREN'S
VERSE

COMPILED BY MARK DANIEL

M
MACMILLAN CHILDREN'S BOOKS

For Pauline

Conceived by Breslich & Foss

This anthology copyright © Mark Daniel 1986

Design © Breslich & Foss 1986

First published in Great Britain in 1986 by Pavilion Books Limited
in association with Michael Joseph Limited

Premier Picturemac edition published 1989 by
Macmillan Children's Books
A division of Macmillan Publishers Limited
London and Basingstoke
Associated companies throughout the world

ISBN 0-333-51037-2

A CIP catalogue record for this book is available from the British Library.

Printed in Hong Kong

All colour pictures are courtesy of
Fine Art Photographic Library, London
Front cover painting by Luigi Chialiva
Back cover painting by Helen Allingham

CONTENTS

ALL CREATURES
GREAT AND SMALL
∽ 7 ∾

SOME OLD FRIENDS
∽ 37 ∾

SWEET DREAMS
∽ 53 ∾

THE POETS
∽ 76 ∾

THE PAINTERS
∽ 78 ∾

INDEX OF FIRST LINES
∽ 79 ∾

ALL CREATURES
GREAT AND SMALL

A LITTLE COCK SPARROW

A little cock sparrow sat on a tree,
Looking as happy as happy could be,
Till a boy came by with his bow and arrow:
Says, he, "I will shoot the little cock sparrow.

"His body will make me a nice little stew,
And perhaps there'll be some for a little pie too."
Says the little cock sparrow, "I'll be shot if I stay,"
So he flapped his wings and flew away.

ANON

FOUR-AND-TWENTY TAILORS

Four-and-twenty tailors went to kill a snail,
The best man among them durst not touch her tail;
She put out her horns like a little Kyloe cow:
Run, tailors, run! or she'll kill you all e'en now.

ANON

THE OWL

When cats run home and light is come
And dew is cold upon the ground,
And the far-off stream is dumb,
And the whirring sail goes round,
And the whirring sail goes round;
Alone and warming in his five wits,
The white owl in the belfry sits.

When merry milkmaids click the latch,
And rarely smells the new-mown hay,
And the cock hath sung beneath the thatch
Twice or thrice his roundelay,
Twice or thrice his roundelay;
Alone and warming his five wits,
The white owl in the belfry sits.

ALFRED, LORD TENNYSON

THE MOUSE AND THE CAKE

A mouse found a beautiful piece of plum cake,
The richest and sweetest that mortal could make;
'Twas heavy with citron and fragrant with spice,
And covered with sugar all sparkling as ice.

"My stars!" cried the mouse, while his eye beamed with glee,
"Here's a treasure I've found: what a feast it will be;
But, hark! there's a noise, 'tis my brothers at play;
So I'll hide with the cake, lest they wander this way.

"Not a bit shall they have, for I know I can eat
Every morsel myself, and I'll have such a treat."
So off went the mouse as he held the cake fast;
While his hungry young brothers went scampering past.

He nibbled, and nibbled, and panted, but still
He kept gulping it down till he made himself ill;
Yet he swallowed it all, and 'tis easy to guess,
He was soon so unwell that he groaned with distress.

His family heard him, and as he grew worse,
They sent for the doctor, who made him rehearse
How he'd eaten the cake to the very last crumb,
Without giving his playmates and relatives some.

"Ah me!" cried the doctor, "advice is too late;
You must die before long, so prepare for your fate.
If you had but divided the cake with your brothers,
'Twould have done you no harm, and been good for the others.

"Had you shared it, the treat had been wholesome enough;
But eaten by *one*, it was dangerous stuff;
So prepare for the worst —" and the word had scarce fled,
When the doctor turned round, the patient was dead.

Now all little people the lesson may take,
And *some* large ones may learn from the mouse and the cake;
Not to be over-selfish with what we may gain,
Or the best of our pleasures may turn into pain.

ELIZA COOK

Eliza Cook's Journal, 1849

CHOOSING THEIR NAMES

Our old cat has kittens three –
What do you think their names should be?

One is tabby with emerald eyes,
And a tail that's long and slender,
And into a temper she quickly flies
   If you ever by chance offend her.
     I think we shall call her this –
     I think we shall call her that –
Now, don't you think that *Pepperpot*
     Is a nice name for a cat?

One is black with a frill of white,
   And her feet are all white fur,
If you stroke her she carries her tail upright
   And quickly begins to purr.
     I think we shall call him this –
     I think we shall call him that –
Now, don't you think that *Sootikin*
     Is a nice name for a cat?

One is a tortoiseshell, yellow and black,
   With plenty of white about him;
If you tease him, at once he sets up his back,
   He's a quarrelsome one, ne'er doubt him.
     I think we shall call her this –
     I think we shall call her that –
Now, don't you think that *Scratchaway*
     Is a nice name for a cat?

Our old cat has kittens three
And I fancy these their names will be:
Pepperpot, Sootikin, Scratchaway – there!
Were ever kittens with these to compare?
And we call the old mother –
    Now what do you think? –
  Tabitha Longclaws Tiddley Wink.

THOMAS HOOD

A Garland of Verses for
Little People, 1866

ALL THINGS BRIGHT
AND BEAUTIFUL

All things bright and beautiful,
　　All creatures great and small,
All things wise and wonderful,
　　The Lord God made them all.

Each little flower that opens,
　　Each little bird that sings,
He made their glowing colours,
　　He made their tiny wings.

The purple-headed mountain,
　　The river running by,
The sunset, and the morning,
　　That brightens up the sky;

The cold wind in the winter,
　　The pleasant summer sun,
The ripe fruits in the garden,
　　He made them every one.

He gave us eyes to see them,
　　And lips that we might tell,
How great is God Almighty,
　　Who has made all things well.

CECIL FRANCES ALEXANDER
Hymns for Little Children, 1848

DONKEY RIDING

Were you ever in Quebec,
Stowing timbers on a deck,
Where there's a king in his golden crown
Riding on a donkey?

Hey ho, and away we go,
Donkey riding, donkey riding,
Hey ho, and away we go,
Riding on a donkey.

Were you ever in Cardiff Bay,
Where the folks all shout, Hooray!
Here comes John with his three months' pay,
Riding on a donkey?

Hey ho, and away we go,
Donkey riding, donkey riding,
Hey ho, and away we go,
Riding on a donkey.

Were you ever off Cape Horn,
Where it's always fine and warm?
See the lion and the unicorn
Riding on a donkey.

Hey ho, and away we go,
Donkey riding, donkey riding,
Hey ho, and away we go,
Riding on a donkey.

ANON

THE DONKEY

When fishes flew and forests walked
    And figs grew upon thorn,
Some moment when the moon was blood,
    Then surely I was born;

With monstrous head and sickening cry
    And ears like errant wings,
The devil's walking parody
    On all four-footed things.

The tattered outlaw of the earth,
    Of ancient crooked will;
Starve, scourge, deride me: I am dumb,
    I keep my secret still.

Fools! For I also had my hour;
    One far fierce hour and sweet:
There was a shout about my ears,
    And palms before my feet!

G. K. CHESTERTON

The Wild Knight, 1900

THE ROBINS

A robin and a robin's son
Once went to town to buy a bun.
They couldn't decide on plum or plain,
And so they went back home again.

ANON

Little Robin Red-breast
Sat upon a rail,
Needle, naddle, went his head,
Wiggle, waggle, went his tail.

ANON

TO A BUTTERFLY

I've watched you now a full half-hour,
Self-poised upon that yellow flower;
And, little butterfly! indeed
I know not if you sleep or feed.
How motionless! Not frozen seas
More motionless! And then
What joy awaits you, when the breeze
Has found you out among the trees,
And calls you forth again!

This plot of orchard-ground is ours;
My trees they are, my sister's flowers;
Here rest your wings when they are weary,
Here lodge as in a sanctuary!
Come often to us, fear no wrong;
Sit near us on the bough!
We'll talk of sunshine and of song,
And summer days, when we are young;
Sweet childish days, that were as long
As twenty days are now.

WILLIAM WORDSWORTH

Poems Founded on the Affections, 1807

TWO LITTLE KITTENS

Two little kittens, one stormy night,
Began to quarrel, and then to fight;
One had a mouse, the other had none,
And that's the way the quarrel begun.

"I'll have that mouse," said the biggest cat;
"You'll have that mouse? We'll see about that!"
"I *will* have that mouse," said the eldest son;
"You *shan't* have the mouse," said the little one.

I told you before 'twas a stormy night
When these two little kittens began to fight;
The old woman seized her sweeping broom,
And swept the two kittens right out of the room.

The ground was covered with frost and snow,
And the two little kittens had nowhere to go;
So they laid them down on the mat at the door,
While the old woman finished sweeping the floor.

Then they crept in, as quiet as mice,
All wet with the snow, and as cold as ice,
For they found it was better, that stormy night,
To lie down and sleep than to quarrel and fight.

ANON

Pussy can sit by the fire and sing,
Pussy can climb a tree,
Or play with a silly old cork and string
to 'muse herself, not me.
But I like Binkie my dog, because
He knows how to behave;
So, Binkie's the same as the first Friend was,
And I am the Man in the Cave.

Pussy will play Man-Friday till
It's time to wet her paw
And make her walk on the window-sill
(For the footprint Crusoe saw);
Then she fluffles her tail and mews,
And scratches and won't attend.
But Binkie will play whenever I choose,
And he is my true first friend.

Pussy will rub my knees with her head
Pretending she loves me hard;
But the very minute I go to bed
Pussy runs out in the yard,
And there she stays till the morning-light;
So I know it is only pretend;
But Binkie, he snores at my feet all night,
and he is my Firstest Friend!

RUDYARD KIPLING

Just So Stories, 1902

I had a little pony
His name was Dapple-grey
I lent him to a lady
To ride a mile away
She whipped him
She slashed him
She rode him through the mire
I'll never let my pony now
For any lady's hire.

ANON

THE COUNTRY MOUSE AND THE CITY MOUSE

In a snug little cot lived a fat little mouse,
Who enjoyed, unmolested, the range of the house;
With plain food content, she would breakfast on cheese,
She dined upon bacon, and supped on grey peas.

A friend from the town to the cottage did stray,
And he said he was come a short visit to pay;
So the mouse spread her table as gay as you please,
And brought the nice bacon and charming grey peas.

The visitor frowned, and he thought to be witty:
Cried he, "You must know, I am come from the city,
Where we all should be shocked at provisions like these,
For we never eat bacon and horrid grey peas.

"To town come with me, I will give you a treat:
Some excellent food, most delightful to eat.
With me shall you feast just as long as you please;
Come, leave this fat bacon and shocking grey peas."

This kind invitation she could not refuse,
And the city mouse wished not a moment to lose;
Reluctant she quitted the fields and the trees,
The delicious fat bacon and charming grey peas.

They slyly crept under a gay parlour door,
Where a feast had been given the evening before;
And it must be confessed they on dainties did seize,
Far better than bacon, or even grey peas.

Here were custard and trifle, and cheesecakes good store,
Nice sweetmeats and jellies, and twenty things more;
All that art had invented the palate to please,
Except some fat bacon and smoking grey peas.

They were nicely regaling, when into the room
Came the dog and the cat, and the maid with a broom:
They jumped in a custard both up to their knees;
The country mouse sighed for her bacon and peas.

Cried she to her friend, "Get me safely away,
I can venture no longer in London to stay;
For if oft you receive interruptions like these,
Give me my nice bacon and charming grey peas.

"Your living is splendid and gay, to be sure,
But the dread of disturbance you ever endure;
I taste true delight in contentment and ease,
And I *feast* on fat bacon and charming grey peas."

RICHARD SCRAFTON SHARPE

Old Friends in a New Dress, 1807

THE BIRD'S NEST

I'd not despoil the linnet's nest
   That whistles on the spray;
I'd not despoil the tuneful lark
   That sings at break of day;
I would not rob the charming thrush
   That chants so sweet at e'en;
Nor would not rob the lovely wren,
   With her bower of green.

The birds – they are like children
   That dance upon the lea;
And they will not sing in cages
   As they do in bush or tree.
They are just like tiny children
   Dear to their mother's heart;
And such as would the treasures steal
   Enact a cruel part!

ANON

Wire, briar, limber-lock,
Three geese in a flock;
One flew east, one flew west,
And one flew over the cuckoo's nest.

ANON

THE THREE LITTLE PIGS

A jolly old sow once lived in a sty,
   And three little piggies had she,
And she waddled about saying "Umph! Umph! Umph!"
   While the little ones said "Wee! wee!"

"My dear little brothers," said one of the brats,
   "My dear little piggies," said he;
"Let us all for the future say, Umph! Umph! Umph!"
   And they *wouldn't* say "Wee! wee! wee!"

So after a time these little pigs died,
   They all died of *felo de se;**
From trying too hard to say "Umph! Umph! Umph!"
   For they only could say "Wee! wee!"

MORAL
A moral there is to this little song,
   A moral that's easy to see;
Don't try when you're young to say "Umph! Umph! Umph!"
   For you only can say "Wee! wee!"

ALFRED SCOTT GATTY

Aunt Judy's Magazine, February 1870

**felo de se,* self-murder

TEN LITTLE MICE

Ten little mice sat in a barn to spin,
Pussy came by, and popped her head in:
What are you at, my jolly ten?
We're making coats for gentlemen.
Shall I come in and cut your threads?
No, Miss Puss, you'd bite off our heads.

ANON

DING DONG BELL

Ding dong bell! Pussy's in the well!
Who put her in? Little Tommy Lin.
Who pulled her out? Little Tommy Stout.
What a naughty boy was that
To drown poor pussy-cat,
Who ne'er did any harm,
But killed all the mice in father's barn.

TRADITIONAL

BIRDS OF A FEATHER

Birds of a feather flock together
And so do pigs and swine,
Rats and mice will have their choice,
And so will I have mine.

ANON

PUSSY

I like little pussy, her coat is so warm;
And if I don't hurt her, she'll do me no harm.
So I'll not pull her tail, nor drive her away,
But pussy and I very gently will play.
She shall sit by my side, and I'll give her some food;
And she'll love me because I am gentle and good.

I'll pat pretty pussy, and then she will purr;
And thus show her thanks for my kindness to her.
But I'll not pinch her ears, nor tread on her paw,
Lest I should provoke her to use her sharp claw.
I never will vex her, nor make her displeased –
For pussy don't like to be worried and teased.

ANON

THE SPIDER AND THE FLY

"Will you walk into my parlour?" said the Spider to the Fly,
"'Tis the prettiest little parlour that ever you did spy;
The way into my parlour is up a winding stair,
And I have many curious things to show when you are there."
"Oh no, no," said the little Fly, "to ask me is in vain,
For who goes up your winding stair can ne'er come down again."

"I'm sure you must be weary, dear, with soaring up so high;
Will you rest upon my little bed?" said the Spider to the Fly.
"There are pretty curtains drawn around, the sheets are fine and thin;
And if you like to rest awhile, I'll snugly tuck you in!"
"Oh no, no," said the little Fly, "for I've often heard it said,
They never, never wake up again, who sleep upon your bed!"

Said the cunning Spider to the Fly, "Dear friend, what can I do,
To prove the warm affection I've always felt for you?
I have within my pantry good store of all that's nice;
I'm sure you're very welcome – will you please to take a slice?"
"Oh no, no," said the little Fly, "kind sir, that cannot be,
I've heard what's in your pantry, and I do not wish to see."

"Sweet creature," said the Spider, "you're witty and you're wise;
How handsome are your gauzy wings, how brilliant are your eyes!
I have a little looking-glass upon my parlour shelf,
If you'll step in a moment, dear, you shall behold yourself."
"I thank you, gentle sir," she said, "for what you're pleased to say,
And bidding you good morning now, I'll call another day."

The Spider turned him round about, and went into his den,
For well he knew the silly Fly would soon come back again;
So he wove a subtle web, in a little corner sly,
And set his table ready, to dine upon the Fly.
Then he came out to his door again, and merrily did sing:
"Come hither, hither, pretty Fly, with the pearl and silver wing;
Your robes are green and purple – there's a crest upon your head;
Your eyes are like the diamond bright, but mine are dull as lead."

Alas, alas! how very soon this silly little Fly,
Hearing his wily, flattering words, came slowly flitting by;
With buzzing wings she hung aloft, then near and nearer drew,
Thinking only of her brilliant eyes, and green and purple hue;
Thinking only of her crested head – poor foolish thing! At last,
Up jumped the cunning Spider, and fiercely held her fast.
He dragged her up his winding stair, into his dismal den,
Within his little parlour – but she ne'er came out again!

MARY HOWITT

The New Year's Gift, 1829

G. Sheridan Knowles
'85

SOME OLD FRIENDS

YOUNG AND OLD

When all the world is young, lad,
  And all the trees are green;
And every goose a swan lad,
  And every lass a queen;
Then hey for boot and horse, lad,
  And round the world away;
Young blood must have its course, lad,
  And every dog his day.

When all the world is old, lad,
  And all the trees are brown;
When all the sport is stale, lad,
  And all the wheels run down;
Creep home, and take your place there,
  The spent and maimed among:
God grant you find one face there,
  You loved when all was young.

CHARLES KINGSLEY
The Water Babies, 1863

THE GINGERBREAD MAN

Smiling girls, rosy boys,
Come and buy my little toys;
Monkeys made of gingerbread,
And sugar horses painted red.

ANON

Sam, Sam, the butcher man,
Washed his face in a frying pan,
Combed his hair with a wagon wheel,
And died with a toothache in his heel.

ANON

Doctor Foster went to Gloucester
In a shower of rain;
He stepped in a puddle,
Right up to his middle,
And never went there again.

ANON

WINIFRED WATERS

Winifred Waters sat and sighed
 Under a weeping willow;
When she went to bed she cried,
 Wetting all her pillow;

Kept on crying night and day,
 Till her friends lost patience;
"What shall we do to stop her, pray?"
 So said her relations.

Send her to the sandy plains
 In the zone called torrid.
Send her where it never rains,
 Where the heat is horrid.

Mind that she has only flour
 For her daily feeding;
Let her have a page an hour
 Of the driest reading –

Navigation, logarithm,
 All that kind of knowledge –
Ancient pedigrees go with 'em
 From the Herald's College.

When the poor girl has endured
 Six months of this drying,
Winifred will come back cured,
 Let us hope, of crying.

WILLIAM BRIGHTY RANDS

Lilliput Lyrics, 1899

THERE WAS AN OLD WOMAN

There was an old woman tossed up in a basket
Nineteen times as high as the moon;
Where she was going I couldn't but ask it,
For in her hand she carried a broom.

"Old woman, old woman, old woman," quoth I,
"Oh whither, Oh whither, Oh whither, so high?"
"To brush the cobwebs off the sky!"
"Shall I go with thee?" "Ay, by-and by."

ANON

THE OLD WOMAN OF NORWICH

There was an old woman, and what do you think?
She lived upon nothing but victuals and drink;
Victuals and drink were the chief of her diet —
Yet this plaguey old woman could never be quiet!

TRADITIONAL

COBBLER, COBBLER

Cobbler, cobbler, mend my shoe,
Get it done by half past two;
Stitch it up, and stitch it down,
Then I'll give you half a crown.

ANON

The lion and the unicorn
Were fighting for the crown;
The lion beat the unicorn
All round the town.
Some gave them white bread,
And some gave them brown;
Some gave them plum cake,
And sent them out of town.

ANON

JEMIMA

There was a little girl, and she had a little curl,
Right in the middle of her forehead,
And when she was good, she was very, very good,
But when she was bad she was horrid.

One day she went upstairs while her parents, unawares,
In the kitchen down below were at their meals,
And she stood upon her head, on her little truckle bed,
And she then began hurraying with her heels.

Her mother heard the noise, and thought it was the boys,
A-playing at a combat in the attic,
But when she climbed the stair and saw Jemima there,
She took her and did spank her most emphatic!

ANON

MARY, MARY...

Mary, Mary, quite contrary,
How does your garden grow?
With silver bells, and cockle-shells,
And pretty maids all in a row.

TRADITIONAL

I am Queen Anne, of whom 'tis said
I'm chiefly famed for being dead,
Queen Anne, Queen Anne, she sits in the sun,
As fair as a lily, as brown as a bun.

ANON

THE QUEEN OF HEARTS

The Queen of Hearts,
She made some tarts,
All on a summer's day,
The Knave of Hearts,
He stole the tarts,
And took them clean away.

The King of Hearts
Called for the tarts
And beat the Knave full sore.
The Knave of Hearts
Brought back the tarts,
And vowed he'd steal no more.

ANON

THE JOLLY MILLER

There was a jolly miller once
Lived on the river Dee;
He worked and sang from morn till night,
No lark more blithe than he.
And this the burden of his song
Forever used to be,
"I care for nobody, no, not I,
And nobody cares for me!"

TRADITIONAL

THE DAUGHTER OF THE FARRIER

The daughter of the farrier
Could find no one to marry her,
Because she said
She would not wed
A man who could not carry her.

The foolish girl was wrong enough,
And had to wait quite long enough;
For as she sat
She grew so fat
That nobody was strong enough.

ANON

MY PRETTY PINK

My pretty little pink, I once did think
That you and I would marry,
But now I've lost all hopes of that,
I can no longer tarry.

I've got my knapsack on my back,
My musket on my shoulder,
To march away to Quebec Town,
To be a gallant soldier.

Where coffee grows on a white-oak-tree,
And the rivers flow with brandy,
Where the boys are like a lump of gold,
And the girls as sweet as candy.

ANON

THE LITTLE MAN AND MAID

There was a little man
And he woo'd a little maid,
And he said, "Little maid, will you wed, wed, wed?
I have little more to say
Than 'will you, yea or nay?'
For least said is soonest mended-ded-ded-ded."

The little maid replied,
(Some say a little sighed,)
"But what shall we have to eat, eat eat?
Will the love that you are rich in
Make a fire in the kitchen?
Or the little god of loving turn the spit, spit spit?"

TRADITIONAL

JOSHUA LANE

"I know I have lost my train,"
Said a man named Joshua Lane;
"But I'll run on the rails
With my coat-tails for sails
And maybe I'll catch it again."

ANON

I had a little nut-tree,
Nothing would it bear
But a silver nutmeg
And a golden pear;
The King of Spain's daughter
She came to visit me,
And all for the sake of my little nut-tree.
I skipped over water,
I danced over sea,
And all the birds in the air couldn't catch me.

ANON

Sing a song of sixpence,
A pocket full of rye;
Four and twenty blackbirds
Baked in a pie!

When the pie was opened
The birds began to sing;
Was not that a dainty dish
To set before the king?

The king was in his counting-house
Counting out his money;
The queen was in the parlour,
Eating bread and honey.

The maid was in the garden,
Hanging out the clothes;
When down came a blackbird
And snapped off her nose.

ANON

SWEET DREAMS

WYNKEN, BLYNKEN AND NOD

Wynken, Blynken and Nod one night
Sailed off in a wooden shoe –
Sailed on a river of crystal light,
Into a sea of dew.
"Where are you going and what do you wish?"
The old moon asked the three.
"We have come to fish for the herring-fish
That live in this beautiful sea;
Nets of silver and gold have we,"
Said Wynken, Blynken, and Nod.

The old moon laughed and sang a song,
As they rocked in the wooden shoe,
And the wind that sped them all night long
Ruffled the waves of dew.
The little stars were the herring-fish
That lived in that beautiful sea –
"Now cast your nets wherever you wish –
But never afeared are we";
So cried the stars to the fishermen three:
Wynken, Blynken and Nod.

All night long their nets they threw
To the stars in the twinkling foam –
Then down from the skies came the wooden shoe,
Bringing the fishermen home;
'Twas all so pretty a sail, it seemed
As if it could not be,
And some folks thought 'twas a dream they'd dreamed
Of sailing the beautiful sea –
But I shall name you the fishermen three:
Wynken, Blynken, and Nod.

Wynken and Blynken are two little eyes,
And Nod is a little head,
And the wooden shoe that sailed the skies
Is a wee one's trundle-bed.
So shut your eyes while mother sings
Of wonderful sights that be,
And you shall see the beautiful things
As you rock on the misty sea,
Where the old shoe rocked the fishermen three:
Wynken, Blynken, and Nod.

EUGENE FIELD

A Little Book of Western Verse, 1889

WINTER TIME

Late lies the wintry sun a-bed,
A frosty, fiery sleepy-head;
Blinks but an hour or two; and then,
A blood-red orange, sets again.

Before the stars have left the skies,
At morning in the dark I rise;
And shivering in my nakedness,
By the cold candle, bathe and dress.

Close by the jolly fire I sit
To warm my frozen bones a bit;
Or with a reindeer-sled, explore
The colder countries round the door.

When to go out, my nurse doth wrap
Me in my comforter and cap,
The cold wind burns my face, and blows
Its frosty pepper up my nose.

Black are my steps on silver sod;
Thick blows my frosty breath abroad;
And tree and house, and hill and lake,
Are frosted like a wedding cake.

ROBERT LOUIS STEVENSON
A Child's Garden of Verses, 1885

WINDY NIGHTS

Whenever the moon and stars are set,
   Whenever the wind is high,
All night long in the dark and wet,
   A man goes riding by.
Late in the night when the fires are out,
Why does he gallop and gallop about?

Whenever the trees are crying aloud,
   And ships are tossed at sea,
By, on the highway, low and loud,
   By at the gallop goes he.
By at the gallop he goes, and then
By he comes back at the gallop again.

ROBERT LOUIS STEVENSON

A Child's Garden of Verses, 1885

NOW THE DAY IS OVER

Now the day is over,
　Night is drawing nigh,
Shadows of the evening
　Steal across the sky.

Now the darkness gathers,
　Stars begin to peep,
Birds and beasts and flowers
　Soon will be asleep.

Jesu, give the weary
　Calm and sweet repose;
With thy tenderest blessing
　May our eyelids close.

Grant to little children
　Visions bright of thee;
Guard the sailors tossing
　On the deep blue sea.

Comfort every sufferer
   Watching late in pain;
Those who plan some evil
   From their sin restrain.

Through the long night-watches
   May thine angels spread
Their white wings above me,
   Watching round my bed.

When the morning wakens,
   Then may I arise
Pure and fresh and sinless
   In thy holy eyes.

Glory to the Father,
   Glory to the Son,
And to thee, blest Spirit,
   Whilst all ages run.

SABINE BARING-GOULD
Hymns Ancient and Modern, 1868

THE CELESTIAL SURGEON

If I have faltered more or less
In my great task of happiness;
If I have moved among my race
And shown no shining morning face;
If beams from happy human eyes
Have moved me not; if morning skies,
Books, and my food, and summer rain
Knocked on my sullen heart in vain:
Lord, thy most pointed pleasure take
And stab my spirit broad awake.

ROBERT LOUIS STEVENSON

Underwoods, 1887

CERTAINTY

I never saw a moor,
I never saw the sea;
Yet know I how the heather looks,
And what a wave must be.

I never spoke with God,
Nor visited in heaven;
Yet certain am I of the spot
As if the chart were given.

EMILY DICKINSON

The Poems, 1855

WHERE DID YOU COME FROM, BABY DEAR?

Where did you come from, baby dear?
Out of the everywhere into here.

Where did you get your eyes so blue?
Out of the sky as I came through.

What makes the light in them sparkle and spin?
Some of the starry spikes left in.

Where did you get that little tear?
I found it waiting when I got here.

What makes your forehead so smooth and high?
A soft hand stroked it as I went by.

What makes your cheek like a warm white rose?
I saw something better than anyone knows.

Whence that three-cornered smile of bliss?
Three angels gave me at once a kiss.

Where did you get this pearly ear?
God spoke, and it came out to hear.

Where did you get those arms and hands?
Love made itself into hooks and bands.

Feet, whence did you come, darling things?
From the same box as the cherubs' wings.

How did they all just come to be you?
God thought about me, and so I grew.

But how did you come to us, you dear?
God thought about you, and so I am here.

GEORGE MACDONALD

At the Back of the North Wind, 1871

THE SNOW

It sifts from leaden sieves,
It powders all the wood,
It fills with alabaster wool
The wrinkles of the road.

It makes an even face
Of mountain and of plain,
Unbroken forehead from the east
Unto the east again.

It reaches to the fence,
It wraps it, rail by rail,
Till it is lost in fleeces;
It flings a crystal veil

On stump and stack and stem,
The summer's empty room,
Acres of seams where harvests were,
Recordless, but for them.

It ruffles wrists of posts,
As ankles of a queen,
Then stills its artisans like ghosts,
Denying they have been.

EMILY DICKINSON

The Poems, 1855

Matthew, Mark, Luke and John,
Bless the bed that I lie on.
If I should die before I wake,
I pray the Lord my soul to take.

ANON

"How many miles is it to Babylon?"
"Three score miles and ten."
"Can I get there by candle-light?"
"Yes, and back again!
If your heels are nimble and light,
You may get there by candle-light."

ANON

A CHRISTMAS CAROL

In the bleak mid-winter
   Frosty wind made moan,
Earth stood hard as iron,
   Water like a stone;
Snow had fallen, snow on snow,
   Snow on snow,
In the bleak mid-winter
   Long ago.

Our God, heaven cannot hold Him,
   Nor earth sustain;
Heaven and Earth shall flee away
   When He comes to reign:
In the bleak mid-winter
   A stable-place sufficed
The Lord God Almighty
   Jesus Christ.

What can I give Him,
   Poor as I am?
If I were a shepherd
   I would bring a lamb;
If I were a wise man
   I would do my part –
Yet what I can, I give Him,
   Give my heart.

CHRISTINA GEORGINA ROSSETTI

Sing-Song, 1872

AN EVENING SCENE

The sheep-bell tolleth curfew time;
　　The gnats, a busy rout,
Fleck the warm air; the dismal owl
　　Shouteth a sleepy shout;
The voiceless bat, more felt than seen,
　　Is flitting round about.

The aspen leaflets scarcely stir;
　　The river seems to think;
Athwart the dusk, broad primroses
　　Look coldly from the brink,
Where, listening to the freshet's noise,
　　The quiet cattle drink.

The bees boom past; the white moths rise
　　Like spirits from the ground;
The gray flies hum their weary tune,
　　A distant, dream-like sound;
And far, far off, to the slumb'rous eve,
　　Bayeth an old guard-hound.

COVENTRY PATMORE

Poems, 1906

THE STAR

Twinkle, twinkle, little star,
How I wonder what you are!
Up above the world so high,
Like a diamond in the sky.

When the blazing sun is gone,
When he nothing shines upon,
Then you show your little light,
Twinkle, twinkle, all the night.

Then the traveller in the dark,
Thanks you for your tiny spark,
He could not see which way to go,
If you did not twinkle so.

In the dark blue sky you keep,
And often through my curtains peep,
For you never shut your eye,
Till the sun is in the sky.

As your bright and tiny spark,
Lights the traveller in the dark –
Though I know not what you are,
Twinkle, twinkle, little star.

JANE TAYLOR

Rhymes for the Nursery, 1806

STAR LIGHT, STAR BRIGHT...

Star light, star bright,
First star I've seen tonight,
Wish I may, wish I might,
Have this wish I wish tonight.

ANON

I see the moon, and the moon sees me.
God bless the moon, and God bless me.

ANON

EVENING

The day is past, the sun is set,
  And the white stars are in the sky;
While the long grass with dew is wet,
  And through the air the bats now fly.

The lambs have now lain down to sleep,
  The birds have long since sought their nests;
The air is still; and dark, and deep
  On the hill side the old wood rests.

Yet of the dark I have no fear,
  But feel as safe as when 'tis light;
For I know God is with me there,
  And He will guard me through the night.

For God is by me when I pray,
  And when I close mine eyes in sleep,
I know that He will with me stay,
  And will all night watch by me keep.

For He who rules the stars and sea,
  Who makes the grass and trees to grow,
Will look on a poor child like me,
  When on my knees I to Him bow.

He holds all things in His right hand,
  The rich, the poor, the great, the small;
When we sleep, or sit, or stand,
  Is with us, for He loves us all.

THOMAS MILLER

Original Poems for My Children, 1850

THE LAND OF NOD

From breakfast on through all the day
At home among my friends I stay,
But every night I go abroad
Afar into the land of Nod.

All by myself I have to go,
With none to tell me what to do –
All alone beside the streams
And up the mountainside of dreams.

The strangest things are there for me,
Both things to eat and things to see,
And many frightening sights abroad
Till morning in the land of Nod.

Try as I like to find the way,
I never can get back by day,
Nor can remember plain and clear
The curious music that I hear.

ROBERT LOUIS STEVENSON

A Child's Garden of Verses, 1885

THE LAND OF STORY-BOOKS

At evening when the lamp is lit,
Around the fire my parents sit;
They sit at home and talk and sing,
And do not play at anything.

Now, with my little gun I crawl
All in the dark along the wall,
And follow round the forest track
Away behind the sofa back.

There, in the night, where none can spy,
All in my hunter's camp I lie,
And play at books that I have read
Till it is time to go to bed.

These are the hills, these are the woods,
These are my starry solitudes;
And there the river by whose brink
The roaring lions come to drink.

I see the others far away.
As if in firelit camp they lay,
And I, like to an Indian scout,
Around their party prowled about.

So, when my nurse comes in for me,
Home I return across the sea,
And go to bed with backward looks
At my dear land of Story-Books.

ROBERT LOUIS STEVENSON

A Child's Garden of Verses, 1885

ROCK-A-BYE BABY...

Rock-a-bye baby,
On the treetop;
When the wind blows,
The cradle will rock;
When the bough breaks,
The cradle will fall;
Down will come cradle,
Baby and all!

TRADITIONAL

ALL THROUGH THE NIGHT

Sleep, my babe, lie still and slumber,
All through the night;
Guardian angels God will lend thee,
All through the night;
Soft and drowsy hours are creeping,
Hill and vale in slumber sleeping,
Mother dear her watch is keeping,
All through the night.

God is here, thou'lt not be lonely,
All through the night;
'Tis not I who guards thee only,
All through the night.
Night's dark shades will soon be over,
Still my watchful care shall hover,
God with me His watch is keeping,
All through the night.

ANON

THE POETS

**ALEXANDER, Cecil Frances
(1818–1895) Ireland**
Born in Co. Wicklow, Ireland. In 1850 she
married the Rev. William Alexander, who was
to become Archbishop of Armagh.
Hymns for Little Children (1848) includes not
only "All Things Bright and Beautiful" but
also "Once in Royal David's City" and "There
is a Green Hill Far Away".

BARING-GOULD, Sabine (1834–1924) UK
Author of "Onward Christian Soldiers" and
159 published works, including novels, travel
books, histories and collections of folk songs.
A rich man by birth, he worked as a curate and
vicar in the churches and mission schools of
Yorkshire before returning to take up living on
his family estates in Devon.

**CHESTERTON, Gilbert Keith
(1874–1936) UK**
Poet, novelist, critic and artist, Chesterton was
extraordinarily prolific. Among his works are
full-length studies of Dickens, Browning,
Stevenson, and St. Thomas Aquinas. He is
principally famous, however, for the Father
Brown stories. A stubborn and formidable
battler with his pen, Chesterton was renowned
in real life for his bumbling absent-
mindedness and his unfailing ability to get
lost.

COOK, Eliza (1818–1889) UK
Eliza Cook started to compose verse before
she was fifteen. Her first published book
appeared in 1835, when she was just seventeen.
She contributed verses to many London
journals – at first anonymously and then, after
the immense success of a poem called "The
Old Arm Chair", openly and profitably.
Eventually, in 1849, she started her own
publication, *Eliza Cook's Journal.* The last issue
was printed in 1854. Her greatest contribution
to literature was that she drew attention to the
forgotten talents of Thomas Hood (q.v.).
Eliza Cook lived in London throughout her
life.

**DICKINSON, Emily Elizabeth
(1830–1886) USA**
The daughter of a wealthy lawyer from
Amherst, Massachusetts, Emily Dickinson
lived the quiet life of a respectable, intellectual
spinster. She had several very intelligent male
friends, but was otherwise a recluse for the
latter twenty-five years of her life. No one
knew until she died that she had written more
than a thousand poems of remarkable
sensitivity and originality. Like the English
naturalist, Gilbert White, she expressed the
sharp, ecstatic pangs occasioned by everyday
things precisely observed. Her images were
eccentric, witty and concise.

FIELD, Eugene (1850–1895) USA
Born in St. Louis, Missouri, Field was a
columnist with the *Chicago Morning News*,
contributing literary and humorous pieces or
light verse. "Wynken, Blynken and Nod" was
written in bed "upon brown wrapping paper"
one night in March 1889 when the entire
poem suddenly came into his head.

GATTY, Alfred Scott (1847–1918) UK
Gatty held the highest heraldic order – Garter
King of Arms (1904). He was also a song
writer and contributed verses to his mother's
Aunt Judy's Magazine.

HOOD, Thomas (1799–1845) UK
Born in London, the son of a Scottish
bookseller and printer, Hood contributed to
magazines and studied engraving before
appointment as sub-editor on the *London
Magazine,* where he met de Quincey, Lamb,
and others. The great parodist John Hamilton
Reynolds became Hood's closest friend and
collaborator, and Hood married his sister. He
edited several magazines and his works
achieved considerable popularity, notably the
Song of the Shirt (1843) and the *Bridge of Sighs*
(1843), which combine the faint tone of pathos
so characteristic of Hood's work and the
jaunty humour which, according to his friends,
he always evinced.

HOWITT, Mary (1799–1888) UK
Née Botham. Wife of author William Howitt
and mother of twelve children. Mary Howitt, a
Quaker, collaborated with her husband and
published more than a hundred books in her
own right. Among other claims to fame, she
was the first English translator of Hans
Christian Andersen.

KINGSLEY, Charles (1819–1875) UK
Born in England at Holne, Dartmoor. Kingsley became rector of Eversley in Hampshire (1844) after a Cambridge education. A novelist, journalist, and historian, he was Professor of Modern History at Cambridge from 1860 to 1869.

KIPLING, (Joseph) Rudyard (1865–1936) UK
Born in Bombay and educated in England, Kipling returned to India in 1882 and rapidly acquired a reputation as a brilliant reporter and satirical poet. He settled in London in 1889. His most popular works include *The Jungle Books* (1894–5), *Stalky and Co.* (1899), *Kim* (1901), and *Just So Stories* (1902). He was a fine wordsmith; "A word," he said, "should fall in its place like a bell in a full chime."

MACDONALD, George (1824–1905) UK
Scottish novelist and poet. Educated at Aberdeen University and at Highbury Congregationalist College where he became a pastor, he is best remembered for *At the Back of the North Wind* (1871), *The Princess and Curdie* (1882), and *The Princess and the Goblin* (1871). Macdonald had eleven children of his own.

MILLER, Thomas (1807–1874) UK
An illiterate English basket-weaver from Nottingham, Miller taught himself to read and write. He had his poems delivered to Lady Blessington in baskets he had made himself. Once she had expressed her approval the rest of London followed suit.

PATMORE, Coventry (1823–1896) UK
Amateur of chemistry, Coleridge scholar and Assistant Keeper of the British Library in London. His best known work, the intimate serial poem "The Angel in the House" (1862) is a celebration of every aspect of married life: Patmore was happily married three times. He restricted himself largely to traditional verse forms but longed to experiment, like Gerard Manley Hopkins (with whom he had a correspondence) with metre.

RANDS, William Brighty (1823–1882) UK
A self-educated children's poet who was born and spent most of his life in or about West London.

ROSSETTI, Christina Georgina (1830–1894) UK
Sister of the poet and painter Dante Gabriel Rossetti, Christina led a sad life and failed to fulfill her early exceptional promise. She twice rejected suitors because of her high Anglican religious principles, and her verses are devout and full of the sadness of "what might have been". Her first collection, *Goblin Market* (1862), was very much her finest, but *Sing-Song* (1872) is full of charming, simple verses for children. She was always frail and, at the time of *Sing-Song's* composition, was very close to death from Grave's disease. Thereafter, she taught with her mother and wrote morally improving verse.

SHARPE, Richard Scrafton (c. 1775–1852) UK
A London grocer who wrote copious comic verse anonymously and only revealed his identity in 1837.

STEVENSON, Robert Louis (1850–1894) UK
A master stylist and supremely imaginative writer who contrived to lead a hero's life despite often crippling illness. All his life he suffered from chronic bronchial problems and acute nervous excitability. Stevenson nonetheless travelled extensively, wrote many fine essays and novels and in *A Child's Garden of Verses* (1885) applied his highly developed gifts of imagination and sympathy to the emotions and enthusiasms of childhood. In so doing he can be said to have invented a whole new genre of verse. In 1888 he travelled in the South Seas and at last settled with his family in Samoa where the natives called him "Tusitala" (the tale-teller). He died there of a brain hemorrhage. His novels include *Treasure Island* (1883), *Kidnapped* (1886), *Catriona* (1893), and, for older readers, the eerie *Strange Case of Dr. Jekyll and Mr. Hyde* (1886).

THE PAINTERS

TAYLOR, Jane (1783–1824) UK
With her sister Ann, Jane Taylor was the best known children's poet of her time. They lived together at their family home in Colchester, Essex.

TENNYSON, Alfred, Lord (1809–1892) UK
Although the most honoured and fêted poet of the Victorian era, Tennyson liked to live "far from the madding crowd" in Hampshire or on the Isle of Wight. He was very prolific and, although he never wrote specifically for children, many of his works have become firm favourites with young people because of their grand romantic subject matter or because they are ideal for reciting.

WORDSWORTH, William (1770–1850) UK
Poet Laureate. He lived at Grasmere in the English Lake District with his sister Dorothy. At his best, as in "The Prelude" or "Tintern Abbey", Wordsworth was a brilliant, thoughtful nature poet; at his worst he was capable of gaucheness and banality.

page
Title   E. Thomas Hale (fl. from 1898)
6   John Frederick Herring (fl. 1860 – 1875)
11   Philip Eustace Stretton (fl. 1884 – 1919)
14   Luigi Chialiva (nineteenth century)
19   Augusta Innes Withers (fl. 1829 – 1865)
21   Albert Durer Lucas (1828 – 1918)
25   Edward Killingworth Johnson (1825 – 1923)
28   Charles Edward Wilson (fl. 1891 – 1936)
29   Luigi Chialiva (nineteenth century)
32   Alexander Koester (1864 – 1932)
33   C. Blair (nineteenth century)
36   George Sheridan Knowles (1863 – 1931)
41   Alexander M. Rossi (fl. 1870 – 1903)
44   Anon.
45   Helen Allingham (1848 – 1926)
48   E. Thomas Hale (fl. from 1898)
49   Frederick Goodall (1822 – 1904)
52   Henry Le Jeune (1819 – 1904)
55   Edward Robert Hughes (1851 – 1914)
58   Fred Hall (1860 – 1948)
62   Joseph Farquharson (1846 – 1935)
67   Edward Ridley (nineteenth century)
71   John Atkinson Grimshaw (1863 – 1893)
74   George Smith (1829 – 1901)

A BRIEF NOTE ON SOME OF THE ANONYMOUS VERSES

The age of some familiar rhymes is consistently surprising. "I Had a Little Nut-tree . . ." for example, refers to the visit of Joanna of Castile to the court of Henry VII in 1506. "Sing a Song of Sixpence" is quoted by Beaumont and Fletcher. "I had a little pony" has been found in various forms, including (c. 1630): "I had a little bonny nagg/his name was Dapple Gray;/And he would bring me to an ale-house/A mile out of my way . . ."

INDEX OF FIRST LINES

A

A jolly old sow once lived in a sty,	30
A little cock sparrow sat on a tree,	8
All things bright and beautiful,	15
A mouse found a beautiful piece of plum cake,	10
A robin and a robin's son	18
At evening when the lamp is lit,	73

B

Birds of a feather flock together	32

C

Cobbler, cobbler, mend my shoe,	43

D

Ding dong bell! Pussy's in the well!	31
Doctor Foster went to Gloucester	39

F

Four-and-twenty tailors went to kill a snail,	8
From breakfast on through all the day	72

H

"How many miles is it to Babylon?"	64

I

I am Queen Anne, of whom 'tis said	46
I'd not despoil the linnet's nest	28
If I have faltered more or less	60
I had a little nut-tree,	50
I had a little pony	24
"I know I have lost my train,"	50
I like little pussy, her coat is so warm;	33
In a snug little cot lived a fat little mouse,	26
I never saw a moor,	60
In the bleak mid-winter	65
I see the moon, and the moon sees me.	69
It sifts from leaden sieves,	63
I've watched you now a full half-hour,	20

L

Late lies the wintry sun a-bed,	56
Little Robin Red-breast	18

M

Mary, Mary, quite contrary,	45
Matthew, Mark, Luke and John,	64
My pretty little pink, I once did think	48

N

Now the day is over,	58

O

Our old cat has kittens three –	12

P

Pussy can sit by the fire and sing,	23

R

Rock-a-bye, baby,	74

S

Sam, Sam, the butcher man,	39
Sing a song of sixpence,	51
Sleep, my babe, lie still and slumber,	75
Smiling girls, rosy boys,	38
Star light, star bright,	69

T

Ten little mice sat in a barn to spin,	31
The day is past, the sun is set,	70
The lion and the unicorn	43
The Queen of Hearts,	46
The sheep-bell tolleth curfew time;	66
The daughter of the farrier	47
There was a jolly miller once	47
There was a little girl, and she had a little curl,	44
There was a little man	49
There was an old woman, and what do you think?	42
There was an old woman tossed up in a basket	42
Twinkle, twinkle, little star,	68
Two little kittens, one stormy night,	22

W

Were you ever in Quebec,	16
When cats run home and light is come	9
When all the world is young, lad,	38
Whenever the moon and stars are set,	57
When fishes flew and forests walked	17
Where did you come from, baby dear?	61
"Will you walk into my parlour?" said the Spider to the Fly,	34
Winifred Waters sat and sighed	40
Wire, briar, limber-lock,	29
Wynken, Blynken and Nod one night	54

Other Premier Picturemacs you will enjoy

A FIRST GOLDEN TREASURY OF CHILDREN'S VERSE
   Compiled by Mark Daniel
A FIRST TREASURY OF FAIRY TALES Edited by Michael Foss
A SECOND TREASURY OF FAIRY TALES Edited by Michael Foss
THE MAGIC OINTMENT Eric Quayle/Michael Foreman
BLACK BEAUTY Anna Sewell/Robin McKinley/Susan Jeffers
THE ENCHANTER'S SPELL Illustrated by Gennady Spirin
THE ENCHANTED WORLD Part One Amabel Williams-Ellis/Moira Kemp
THE ENCHANTED WORLD Part Two Amabel Williams-Ellis/Moira Kemp

For a complete list of Picturemac and Premier Picturemac
titles write to:

Macmillan Children's Books,
18–21 Cavaye Place, London SW10 9PG